# Daily Life in ANCIENT ROME

Don Nardo

raintree

a Capstone company — publishers for children

Raintree is an imprint of Capstone Global Library Limited, a company incorporated in England and Wales having its registered office at 7 Pilgrim Street, London, EC4V 6LB – Registered company number: 6695582

www.raintreepublishers.co.uk
myorders@raintreepublishers.co.uk

Text © Capstone Global Library Limited 2015
First published in hardback in 2015
The moral rights of the proprietor have been asserted.

Edited by Clare Lewis and Catherine Neitge
Designed by Philippa Jenkins
Original illustrations © Capstone Global Library Limited 2015
Illustrated by Roger@KJA-artists.com
Picture research by Jo Miller
Production by Helen McCreath
Originated by Capstone Global Library Ltd
Printed and bound in China

ISBN 978 1 406 28806 3
18 17 16 15 14
10 9 8 7 6 5 4 3 2 1

**British Library Cataloguing in Publication Data**
A full catalogue record for this book is available from the British Library.

**Acknowledgements**
We would like to thank the following for permission to reproduce photographs: Alamy: Heritage Image Partnership Ltd/Werner Forman Archive, 12, 35, Image Asset Management Ltd., 20, Lebrecht Music and Arts Photo Library, 28, Martin Shields, 19, North Wind Picture Archives, 30, 39; Corbis: Araldo de Luca, 14, 23, National Geographic Society/ Herbert M. Herget, 37, Vanni Archive, 31; Getty Images: Culture Club, 18, De Agostini /DEA Picture Library/A. Dagli Orti, 24, De Agostini/DEA Picture Library, 10, The Bridgeman Art Library/Herbert M. Herget, 8, 26; Mary Evans Picture Library: Illustrated London News Ltd, 29; Newscom: 20TH CENTURY FOX/Album, 32, Oronoz/Album, 34, Prisma/Olimpia Torres/ Album, 16, Robert Harding/John Ross, 6, VWPics/Paulo Amorim, 40, World History Archive, 33; Shutterstock: irisphoto1, 22, John Copland, cover, Renata Sedmakova, 7, WitR, 5, worradirek, 41; UIG via Getty Images: LTL, 36
Design Elements: Nova Development Corporation, clip art (throughout), Shutterstock: imanolqs

We would like to thank Professor Ray Laurence for his help in the preparation of this book.

Every effort has been made to contact copyright holders of material reproduced in this book. Any omissions will be rectified in subsequent printings if notice is given to the publisher.

All the Internet addresses (URLs) given in this book were valid at the time of going to press. However, due to the dynamic nature of the Internet, some addresses may have changed, or sites may have changed or ceased to exist since publication. While the author and publisher regret any inconvenience this may cause readers, no responsibility for any such changes can be accepted by either the author or the publisher.

# CONTENTS

Some words are shown in bold, **like this**. You can find out what they mean by looking in the glossary.

The ancient Romans were one of the most successful peoples in history. Their nation lasted from about 750 **BC** to **AD** 476 – more than 1,200 years! During those years, their armies conquered one country after another. At its height, in the 200s AD, the Roman Empire covered much of Europe. It also included Britain, North Africa and parts of the Middle East.

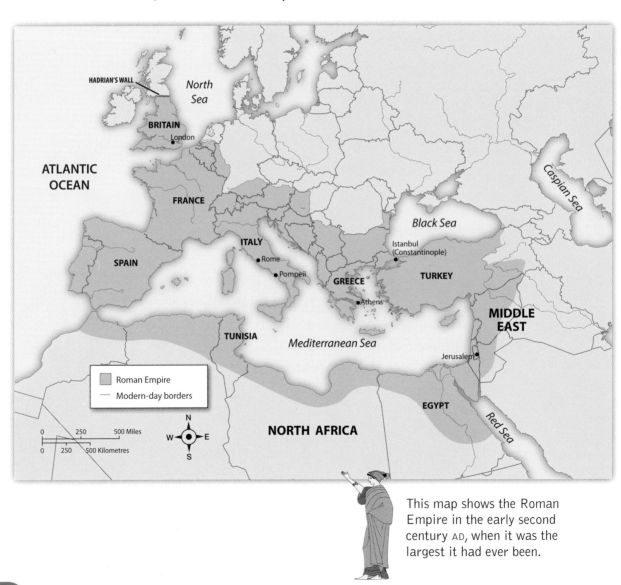

HADRIAN'S WALL
*North Sea*
BRITAIN
• London
ATLANTIC OCEAN
FRANCE
*Black Sea*
*Caspian Sea*
ITALY
Istanbul (Constantinople)
SPAIN
• Rome
• Pompeii
GREECE
TURKEY
• Athens
MIDDLE EAST
TUNISIA
*Mediterranean Sea*
Jerusalem •
Roman Empire
Modern-day borders
EGYPT
*Red Sea*
0   250   500 Miles
0   250   500 Kilometres
N W E S
NORTH AFRICA

This map shows the Roman Empire in the early second century AD, when it was the largest it had ever been.

This stone arch was built to celebrate a military victory, and still survives today.

## A talent for the practical

This remarkable achievement occurred for several reasons. One was that the Romans had an amazing talent for solving practical problems. Also, they regularly applied that ability to building things. Roman painters, sculptors, and musicians created some wonderful works. But the true Roman artist was an **engineer**, or master builder. Rome's world empire was created as much by its engineers as by its armies.

The Romans were also great borrowers. Often they chose the best ideas of other peoples and cleverly adapted them to their own needs. A good example was the *scutum*, the rectangular shield used by Rome's soldiers. The early Romans adapted it from a neighbouring Italian people, the Samnites. Rome also borrowed many religious and artistic ideas from the Greeks.

The Romans were determined to win and survive at all costs. The second-century BC Greek writer Polybius noticed this. He told of "how spirited and daring the Romans are when they are determined to do a thing".

Each new generation of Romans led their daily lives in a society that strongly emphasized being practical and determined. The result was that Romans, rich and poor, young and old, became flexible and strong as a people. So Rome's civilization was successful and long lasting.

# HOW DID SOCIAL STATUS IN ROME AFFECT PEOPLE'S LIVES?

From 30 BC to AD 476, Rome's lands were called the Roman Empire. The Empire was ruled by a long series of very powerful leaders, called emperors.

The Empire reached its height of power and influence in its first 200 years. In that time, most emperors were thoughtful and effective. Only a few, like the cruel, murderous Nero, were poor rulers. Most of Rome's residents led safe, happy lives.

## The privileged few

Yet some people were happier, or at least more fortunate, than others. At the top of the social ladder was the emperor. And just below him were two groups of nobles.

### THE FIRST EMPEROR

The first, most famous, and arguably greatest Roman emperor was Augustus. Born in 63 BC, when Rome was a **republic** run by elected leaders, he was known as Octavian. He rose to power during a period of bloody **civil wars**. In 30 BC, he emerged as both victor and sole commander of Rome's huge military. Seeing no other choice, the nobles accepted his authority and renamed him Augustus. Although he never called himself emperor, he was in fact the first of many.

Cicero was a powerful politician, writer and speaker.

The emperor and nobles made up only a tiny fraction of Rome's population. Yet they largely controlled society. They also led lives of luxury, with many servants. Partly, such high **social status** came from tradition. It had long been thought that nobles were better than commoners.

Tradition also claimed that men were cleverer than women. With some exceptions, therefore, Roman men controlled the lives of their wives, mothers and daughters.

## Clients and patrons

Commoners, or plebs, made up the bulk of the Empire's population. They were mostly people of modest or poor means, such as farmers.

The commoners' low social status worked against them in several ways. The most visible one was a social system called **patronage**. In it, a commoner, the **client**, and a noble, the **patron**, had an arrangement. In theory, it was supposed to benefit both. But the wealthy and influential patron usually got more from the relationship. Some clients took part in the arrangement one or two days a week, while others did so almost every

People of all social classes mill about in Rome's port town of Ostia. A rich patron usually walked along with several of his clients.

## HOW DO WE KNOW?

### The decent patron

Some patrons treated their clients rudely. Such a person might keep them waiting for hours. Or he might demand much from them and give little in return. Such bad behaviour is known because the Roman noble and playwright Seneca the Younger wrote about it.

day.

Such a day began early in the morning with the *salutatio*, or "morning salute". The client washed and put on fresh clothes. He then walked to his patron's home. There, the client politely greeted the patron. The patron then explained the favours he wanted the client to perform that day. For example, the patron might take him and other clients along with him on social calls. This was because travelling with a group of loyal followers enhanced the patron's reputation. If he had to make a speech or appear in court, he would bring along as many clients as possible. They would frequently clap and cheer for him, making him look more impressive.

In return for such favours, the client might receive a bit of money. But a much better reward was an invitation to dine at the patron's house. Besides free food, the client got to socialize with people of a higher social status.

# WHAT KIND OF HOUSES DID THE ROMANS LIVE IN?

The size and quality of a Roman's house depended on its owner's income and social status. The emperors lived in huge palaces with many rooms and hundreds of servants. And the nobles had large, comfortable townhouses. They also had large country houses called **villas**.

This cut-away drawing shows a wealthy Roman home. The large area with the tiled floor and square-shaped pool is the atrium.

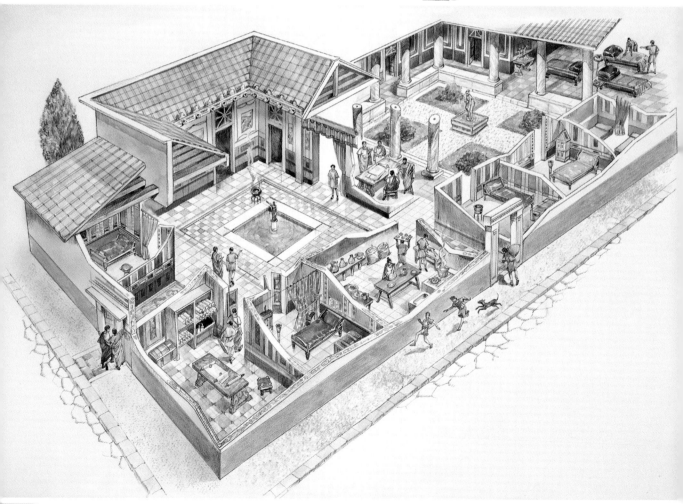

## Homes of the rich and famous

These townhouses and villas were usually made of brick. Most often they were built around an inner courtyard that was open to the sky. Various rooms lined or led to the courtyard. The house's entrance hall, the **atrium**, was usually decorated with tiled flooring, statues and wall paintings. Also common in the atrium was a small **shrine** where family members prayed.

One or more corridors led from the atrium to the courtyard and other rooms. These included a kitchen, dining area, a few bedrooms and a study used mainly by the father. There were also some small servants' quarters and sometimes a bathroom. The bathroom frequently had stone channels that carried toilet waste to the city's **sewers**. Most bathrooms lacked baths because a majority of Romans preferred bathing in public bathhouses.

More often than not, townhouses and villas had pleasant gardens. This was because all Romans loved nature. When gardening, some Romans got the family slaves to help them, but others preferred to do it themselves.

## HADRIAN'S VAST VILLA

Not surprisingly, the biggest and most luxurious Roman villa was built for an emperor. That ruler, Hadrian, reigned from AD 118 to 138. Located at Tivoli, then not far from Rome, it was not a single structure. It included Hadrian's vast living quarters, a bathhouse, two theatres and several gardens. Evidence shows that Hadrian himself designed some of the villa's luxuries.

# Furniture

By modern standards, ancient Roman townhouses and villas did not have much furniture. Yet they had a stylish, elegant look. Because their owners were wealthy, the houses featured large-scale wall paintings. There were also statues and **mosaics**. The most common piece of furniture was a couch with a padded seat and soft pillows. Small round, three-legged tables frequently stood beside the couches and chairs. Beds had a wooden frame covered by a mattress of cloth stuffed with feathers or wool.

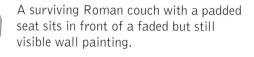

A surviving Roman couch with a padded seat sits in front of a faded but still visible wall painting.

## GLASS AND WINDOWS

For many centuries, Roman windows had no transparent, or see-through, glass. People stretched sheepskin or oil cloth over them. Or they installed glass that was milky or blurry. Around AD 50, however, transparent glass became widely available. But it was expensive, so only the wealthy could afford it.

Less wealthy people owned many of the same items, except that they were rarely padded. The mattresses were more cheaply made and often lacked frames. Bedrooms in all but the very poorest homes also had one or more wooden chests for storage.

## Lighting and heating

People of all social classes used candles and pottery or metal lamps. The lamps burned olive oil or other vegetable oils. Some lamps sat on tables, while others hung from ceilings.

When needed, heat came from a **hypocaust**. It was invented in about 100 BC by a merchant called Gaius Sergius Orata. Beneath a room to be heated was a brick-lined hollow space about 60 centimetres (2 feet) deep. It connected to a fire-burning furnace just outside the house. The heated air from the furnace drifted into the space, warming the floor. The most complex versions had similar spaces inside the walls. Hypocausts were expensive to install. So, with a few exceptions, they were found mainly in upper-class houses.

## Lower-class homes

The homes of Roman commoners were modest compared to those of the wealthy. Farmers' huts were often pieced together with stones or mud-bricks and thatch (bundled tree branches). They had one or two small rooms with dirt floors. And there were few, if any, pieces of furniture. A central hearth provided heat and a place to cook. Family members got their water from the nearest stream or pond.

This is a model of the first three floors of a real apartment block that once stood at the foot of Rome's Capitoline Hill.

In contrast, poor people in Rome and other cities lived mainly in *insulae*. These inexpensive, crowded blocks of flats were made of concrete, bricks, wood and plaster. And they stood from three to six or more storeys high.

Typical flats had one or two tiny rooms. They had no running water, so people had to fill buckets at a nearby public fountain and carry them up several flights of stairs.

The poet Juvenal lived in such a flat in the Subura. It was the city of Rome's most heavily populated neighbourhood. Juvenal described it, saying it was a dangerous place to live. From time to time, some insulae collapsed, killing and injuring many. No one deserved to have "his house collapsing about his ears," he complained. The typical **tenement** "is poised like a house of cards [about] to collapse".

## THE RISK OF FIRES

The inhabitants of the *insulae* used oil lamps to light their flats, so the risk of fires was high. Juvenal claimed that "fires and midnight panics" were common. "By the time the smoke's got up to your third-floor apartment," he said, "your downstairs neighbour is roaring for water!"

The ancient Romans ate many of the same foods that people eat today. However, the manner in which they cooked and ate them was different. Most cooking was done on open hearths lined with bricks or stone. Typically, a hearth was located in the kitchen. An iron grid mounted on top provided a surface for placing cooking pots.

This reconstruction shows how the kitchen in a Roman house would have looked.

## Cooking in the city

Cooking on a hearth worked fine in ground-floor homes. The problem was that most city-dwellers lived higher up in the multi-storeyed *insulae*. Equipping all those flats with charcoal-burning hearths was too dangerous. It would have caused too many fires.

So the wealthy owners of the ground floors of city dwellings were the only people who could cook and eat in on a regular basis. And only they could throw dinner parties with home-cooked food. The far more common poorer people could have a cold breakfast at home. But for a hot meal, they had to go out to eat.

## Common meals

Whether they ate in or out, most Romans ate a light breakfast of bread and sometimes cheese or fruit. Typical lunches included salad, bread and fruit.

Dinner, or *cena*, was the main meal. Common meats included lamb, poultry, fish and the Romans' favourite, pork. Also frequently eaten were stews that mixed meats with vegetables like carrots, onions and cabbage. Usual desserts included nuts, fruit, pudding, cake and other pastries.

## COMMON DRINKS

Most Romans drank wine, which they mixed with water. Indeed, people saw drinking unmixed wine as very bad mannered. Adding honey to wine created another popular drink called mulsum. Some people in the Empire's northern provinces also drank beer.

This modern picture shows Romans feasting in the garden while musicians play.

## Going out for dinner

Those city-living Romans without cooking facilities in their homes had several options. One was to buy items that would keep for a few days. Examples were bread, cheese and fruit. Cheese, fruit and other food items were sold in open-air marketplaces. Bread came from small bakeries, of which there were many in the average city.

## POLITE DINING

At normal meals, most Romans sat upright on chairs, as people do today. At upscale dinner parties, however, diners rested on their sides on couches. The couches were assigned by the host. The higher one's social status, the closer the diner sat to the host.

After the food was served, the guests ate it with their fingers. However, there were exceptions for items like soup and pudding. Diners used spoons for those. Also, the guests usually brought their own napkins, which doubled as "doggy bags". A diner wrapped his leftovers in a napkin and took them home.

### Hundreds of snack bars

**Modern experts know a lot about Roman *thermopolii*. This is because the remains of more than 200 of them were unearthed at Pompeii. That small city, on Italy's western coast, was buried in ash during a volcanic eruption in AD 79.**

Another alternative was to go out for a quick meal. Roman cities had many small snack bars (or cook shops) called *thermopolii*. Each had a wide bar or counter that was open to the pavement. The counter had a small metal grill for cooking meat, stew and soup. Like modern barbecues, the grill rested above a charcoal fire. There were also a number of pottery containers recessed into the counter. Some kept already cooked food warm. Others held uncooked items, such as raw vegetables, cheese, pastries and fruits.

Snack bars sold wine, as did taverns. The taverns served mostly the same foods that snack bars did, but were a bit larger. A tavern also had a few tables and chairs so that customers could sit and eat. Bigger still were formal restaurants. They had huge menus, along with one or more dining rooms with tables and chairs.

This Roman snack bar was discovered in Pompeii.

Roman family life was, like Roman society, male-dominated. Men usually made most of the important decisions for their wives and children. However, wives' position in the family, and women's rights in general, did improve over time.

This 19th century painting shows a Roman father and head of his household, on the right, along with members of his family.

## Fathers and the Family Women

The father and husband in a Roman family was called the **paterfamilias**. The husband controlled all the family property. And only he could file for divorce. The wife's roles were to raise the children and manage the home.

But by the early years of the Empire, women could inherit and control their own property. They could also ask for divorce. In fact, divorces were very common and easy to obtain throughout the Empire period. Also, most wives now had a say in how the family's money was spent.

## Arranging marriages

Wives almost certainly advised their husbands in arranging their children's marriages. Young men and women usually did not choose who they would marry on their own. Instead, the fathers of a boy and girl would agree that those young people should become engaged. Girls could be engaged at the age of seven and married at the age of twelve. However, most girls waited at least until their mid-teenage years to get married. The boy was typically a bit older when he got married – in his late teenage years or early twenties.

 ### HOW DO WE KNOW?

### Deeply in love

Many men deeply loved and respected their wives. This is known partly because the letters of a nobleman, Pliny the Younger, have survived. He addressed one to his wife, Calpurnia, when she was away. "You cannot believe how much I miss you," he wrote. "I love you so much [that] I stay awake most of the night thinking of you."

# Having children

One of the central activities of Roman family life was having children. It was important to have children to inherit the family's property. Couples also had children at least partly to take care of them in their old age. People who were unable to have children often adopted.

## TO KEEP OR REJECT A CHILD?

When a new baby arrived, a Roman father decided whether to keep or reject it. A common reason for rejection was deformity or some other handicap. In that case, the Romans left the infant outside to die. However, quite a few of these abandoned children were rescued by childless couples. This was the theme of a famous Roman myth. In the story, Rome's future founders, Romulus and Remus, were left to die. But a female wolf found and nursed them. Later, a shepherd and his wife raised the boys.

This sculpture shows a she-wolf caring for Rome's founders, Romulus and Remus.

This ancient Roman toy originally had a string that passed through the hole in the horse's nose. The child used the string to pull the toy along the floor.

Roman children were almost always born at home. Most babies were delivered by a **midwife**, usually helped by the women of the household. Usually, a woman delivered her child sitting in an upright position in a special birthing chair. A ceremony to name the infant took place nine days later.

## Playing with toys

As they grew older, children played with toys. Many toys were similar to modern ones. Girls had dolls, along with dollhouses, and boys had miniature wagons and chariots. Girls and boys enjoyed hoops, tops, seesaws, swings and marbles. Children also played with and took care of family pets. Just like today, many families had dogs and cats. It was also common to keep ducks, mice, snakes, pigeons and other birds.

## Getting an education

During the early Empire, parents had to pay for their children to go to school, so only children from families that could afford it went to a primary school, or *ludus*. Both boys and girls attended from the age of seven. They learned basic reading and writing skills. But after three or four years, girls had to leave school to start preparing for marriage.

In this ancient Roman sculpture, a teacher holding a writing board is surrounded by his students.

Boys, meanwhile, continued on to secondary school. There, they studied history, geography, geometry, music and sometimes Greek. A few young men went on to learn **rhetoric** (public speaking) from private tutors. This skill was essential for men who wanted to enter one of Rome's two most celebrated professions – politics and law.

In contrast, most children from poor families never went to school. This is why many Romans were unable to read or write. Those young people usually began working at an early age. In the countryside, both boys and girls helped their parents by doing farm and household chores. In the cities, a boy started learning his father's trade or became an apprentice to another adult worker. A girl learned from her mother or other family women how to cook and make clothes.

## WRITING MATERIALS

Paper was made from **papyrus**, a marsh plant that grew mainly in Egypt. People joined together separate sheets to make rolls about 9 metres (30 feet) long. Each roll was called a book. People wrote on papyrus with a pen made from a river reed or from bronze. They dipped the pen's tip into ink made from soot. Pupils or writers also used thin sheets of wood called leaf-tablets. People could write directly on the wood or cover it with wax and press a pointed object into the wax.

Rome had the largest number of slaves in human history. One third of the population of Italy was made up of slaves. These were non-citizens who had no personal freedom. The masters who owned them forced them to do various kinds of work. Most slaves' jobs were difficult, boring and sometimes dangerous. Household slaves cleaned, cooked, did repairs and ran errands. Farm slaves cleared land, planted crops and herded animals. And public slaves – those owned by the government – cleaned the streets, dug ditches, toiled in mines and helped government officials.

## Slaves everywhere

During the early Empire, there were two main sources of slaves. One was "breeding" them by allowing existing slaves to have children. The other source was buying new slaves from slave markets.

Poorer homes had few or no slaves because they could not afford to feed and house them. In richer families, there were probably five to ten slaves. Very wealthy Roman homes had 50, 80 or even hundreds of slaves, depending on the owners' incomes. It was said that a rich man called Gaius Caelius Isidorus had 4,116 slaves! And each emperor owned three or four times that number.

One reason that Roman society had so many slaves was that slavery was seen as natural. People viewed it as a simple fact of life and believed the gods themselves accepted it. Even most slaves felt this way. Indeed, many slaves who gained their freedom soon purchased their own slaves. The slave owner Isidorus, mentioned above, was a former slave himself!

## The dream of freedom

Many Roman slaves hoped to better their social position in life. The only way slaves could do so was to gain their freedom. A few tried escaping or employing violence, but this approach always failed. The Roman army eventually crushed all slave revolts.

This modern drawing shows Roman slaves tending to furnaces that were used to heat Rome's larger homes and public buildings.

There was another path to freedom, however. It was **manumission**, being freed by one's owner. A slave thereby became a **freedman**, or former slave. A few slaves became free as a gesture of thanks from a kind owner for years

In the Roman countryside, many slaves worked on farms, where they helped with planting, harvesting, feeding animals and cleaning barns and stables.

of loyal service. Or genuine feelings of love might lead to manumission. Also, some slaves managed to buy their freedom. Most household slaves received little gifts of money, like tips, for constant hard work and loyalty. They could spend the money any way they liked. If their masters were willing to allow it, that included saving up to buy their freedom.

Only a small number of Roman slaves were able to gain their freedom in these ways. Some slaves did not earn tips for their labours. Others did not earn enough, and still others had masters unwilling to free them for any reason. Yet that minority who did gain freedom affected how Roman society operated. Former slaves often took jobs that freeborn Romans did not want. Also, some freedmen were talented and hardworking. They did well in a wide range of jobs.

# THE FAILED SLAVE REBELLIONS

Three large-scale slave revolts took place before Augustus established the Empire. The last and most famous was the rebellion of Spartacus, between 73 and 71 BC. While training at a gladiator school, Spartacus escaped along with some others. They freed other slaves and trained them to fight. Spartacus defeated several small Roman armies. But the government finally sent a large one, which crushed the slaves. After that, there were no more Roman slave revolts.

A legend claimed that just before Spartacus's last battle, he killed his horse. He said that if he won he could have any horse in Rome.

The Romans' most common form of relaxation was going to the public baths. In Rome's early centuries, most people did not bathe very often. And when they did, they washed in a river or stream.

## Bathhouses

Roman bathing habits changed over time, however, mainly due to the influence of Greek culture. The Greeks had public bathhouses, and by the time Augustus died in AD 14, bathhouses could be found across the Roman lands. The city of Rome alone then had more than 170 of them. The reason so many bathhouses were needed is that almost everyone – men, women, rich and poor – used them on a regular basis. In fact, most people went at least a few times a week.

BATHS OF CARACALLA.

This 19th century painting of the Baths of Caracalla, in Rome, captures the place's incredible size and grandeur.

This gap in the floor of a Roman building reveals part of the system used for heating bathhouses and other structures.

## Thermae

The first Roman bathhouses were small. But during the Empire, the government built several enormous ones. Called *thermae*, they could hold thousands of bathers at the same time. Each of the *thermae* had a number of rooms containing pools in which people lounged and washed. Some pools were hot, others cold. And the custom was to go from cold to hot or vice versa.

However, the larger bathhouses were not simply places to get clean. They also had exercise rooms and ball courts to help people keep fit. In addition, there were reading rooms, hair salons and snack bars. And many people simply went to the baths to meet friends.

## MEN AND WOMEN BATHERS

Most Romans viewed it as improper for men and women to bathe together in public. So some bathhouses offered separate rooms for women. In others, men and women bathed at different times of the day.

# The public games

Most Romans felt that nothing could beat the public games. Firstly, they were huge in scale and exciting. Secondly, admission was free.

Attended by people from all walks of life, the games were held in two main settings. One was an **amphitheatre**, a large oval-shaped stadium. The largest amphitheatre in Rome was the famous Colosseum. It held roughly 50,000 spectators.

The amphitheatre games featured fights between people and animals. There were also trained animal acts. But the highlight of these games was armed combat among gladiators. Trained to fight to the death, they were mostly slaves. But a few free Romans became gladiators to gain fame or experience the thrill of danger. If one fighter wounded or gained control of his opponent, a decision had to be made. Would the downed man live or die? The leading official present sometimes allowed the spectators to help make that decision. Through shouted words and various hand signals, they called for the beaten gladiator to be spared or killed.

A scene from the 1954 film *Demetrius and the Gladiators* shows a group of gladiators saluting the emperor Caligula on the platform in the distance.

This famous painting from 1882 captures the excitement of the contests held in the Circus Maximus.

## The circus

The other major games venue was the circus, a massive and very long racetrack. The Empire's biggest was the Circus Maximus in Rome. It was 610 metres (2,000 feet) long and 213 metres (700 feet) wide. There, some 250,000 spectators watched chariot races. The most common chariot was drawn by four horses. The most successful charioteer on record was Pompeius Muscosus, with 3,559 victories!

## MANY TYPES OF GLADIATORS

There were many different gladiator types. One had little armour and fought with a net and trident, a long three-pronged spear. Another wore heavy armour and brandished a sword and shield. Still other kinds of gladiators fought with two swords, on horseback or in moving chariots. There were even fighters who clashed while wearing helmets with no eye-holes! They had to search for each other using only sounds and touching. Female gladiators sometimes fought, too.

The Romans were a deeply religious people who worshipped many gods. The relationship between a person and the gods was a sort of bargain. People carried out the traditional sacred **rituals**. In return, the gods showed those worshippers favour. But if a person failed to do his religious duty, the gods might punish him.

People often worshipped daily at home at small shrines. These existed in the atrium or courtyard in larger homes and in almost any room in a poorer house. Many people also attended public ceremonies that took place on religious holidays. These rituals were carried out by official Roman priests.

This bronze figurine of Jupiter, the leader of the Roman gods, once held a thunderbolt in its raised hand and a sceptre in the other.